Fly, Fly, Fly Little Birdy!

By Jacob Monroe

ISBN: 978-1-7355019-0-1 (Paperback)
ISBN: 978-1-7355019-2-5 (Hardback)
ISBN: 978-1-7355019-1-8 (eBook)

For Sophia.
Don't forget to stop by the nest
every once in a while.

Today is Birdy's birthday
She just hatched from her egg
Her eyes will want to open
as she tries to move her legs

She sees the world around her
With trees and bees and plants
She looks around and looks right up
And sees her happy parents

Birdy's one month old now
And can move and see just fine
She's even asked her parents
Can you teach me how to fly?

She tries and tries and tries some more
It's harder than it seems
And when she thinks she's tried too hard
She's flying with her wings!

She flies up high above the park
Far away from where she's from
She sees new things she's never seen
What fun this has become!

Flying further than she planned

She comes across new things

They're big and small and oddly shaped

And most do not have wings!

Quite some time along the way
Birdy makes new friends
They fly with her and run along
And search for hidden gems

When Birdy wants to fly some more
her friends lay down and rest
They say goodbye and sing a song
And wish her all the best

Moving fast and flying high
This bird has seen it all
Volcanoes, trees and lovely friends
A place called Montreal!

A pretty world to live in

For Birdy to explore

But just one thing was on her mind

She hadn't thought before

She left her home in such a rush
She did not say goodbye
She turns around to fly straight home
Before she starts to cry

But wait a minute, wait right there
I think I know this place
That tower and that boat
that green statue with the face!

She flies up high to look around
And searches for her nest
She sees the trees and bees again
And flies her very best!

She finds her tree and looks to see
Her parents' happy smile
She hugs them big and tells her tale
As they listen all the while

The End

Made in the USA
Middletown, DE
02 July 2021